Well Said

Children's Words of Wisdom

Bridget Haase, o.s.u.

ST. ANTHONY MESSENGER PRESS

Cincinnati, Ohio

PHOTOGRAPHY:

Jean-Claude Lejeune: *front cover; pages 2, 4-5, 11, 14-15, 26, 28-29, 36, 43, 47, 50-51, 54, 60-61, 64, 67, 70-71, 75, 78, 80-81, 85, 88, 90*. Copyright ©Jean-Claude Lejeune

James Carroll: *pages iii, 8*. Copyright ©Brand X Pictures

Harry Cutting: *back cover; page 57*. Copyright ©Harry Cutting

Meg Dierkes: *pages 19, 23*. Copyright ©Meg Dierkes

Digital Vision: *page 33*. Copyright ©Digital Vision/PictureQuest

Jim Arbogast: *pages 38-39*. Copyright ©PhotoDisc/Getty Images

Photographs are independent of writing in this book: photographs do not illustrate incidents, events or characters depicted in the writing; writing is not intended to describe incidents, events or characters depicted in photographs.

Cover and book design by Mary Alfieri
Production assistance by Mark Sullivan

Library of Congress Cataloging-in-Publication Data

Well said : children's words of wisdom / [compiled by] Bridget Haase.
    p. cm.
 ISBN 0-86716-475-1
 1. Children--Quotations. I. Haase, Bridget, 1942-
 PN6328.C5 H229 2002
 305.23--dc21

                                    2001008401

ISBN 0-86716-475-1

Published by St. Anthony Messenger Press
www.AmericanCatholic.org
Printed in the U.S.A.

Dedication

To my mother and my father,
whose lives speak well
of faith in their children

Contents

Acknowledgments

I would like to thank:

Albert Haase, O.F.M., Beijing, the People's Republic of China, for his expertise, editorial assistance and brotherly encouragement;

Patricia A. Finn for the final preparation of this manuscript and the staff of St. Brendan's School, Dorchester, Massachusetts, for their enthusiasm and dedication;

Francis Philip Haase, New Orleans, Louisiana, and the late Mary Ann Holthaus, O.S.U., St. Louis, Missouri, for the impetus to begin this book;

and the Ursuline Community, Dedham, Massachusetts, for their devoted and loving support.

Introduction

Most of my life I have been in school. My classrooms have extended from the hollows of Appalachia and villages of Mexico to the desert of Sudan and bush of Senegal. I have taught in a children's center in a maximum-security prison, in a day care for toddlers living with HIV/AIDS, and in inner-city schools and suburban academies. Yet, teacher though I've been, it has been my students who have both taught and inspired me with a wisdom long forgotten behind my curriculum guide and teacher's desk.

Over the years I have collected children's random thoughts, poetic and humorous, insightful and provocative. They have given me cause to pause and to ponder my own life. Now I am doing my homework by sharing these children's lives, their words of wisdom and the lessons learned.

Maren, a fifth grader, inspired the title of this book.

Several years ago, my class was presenting creative ways for peer motivation. After many presentations that far exceeded the five-minute limit, Maren's turn came.

Facing the class with her usual hesitancy and shyness, she waited for encouragement and a little verbal nudge. She took a breath and then declared, in the unmistakable rhythm of poetry, "Remember! / When you have advice to sell, / Speak a little; say it well."

Then she smiled broadly, bowed slightly and sat down.

"Remember!
When you have advice to sell,
Speak a little; say it well."

—MAREN, 11

May these children's words, well said, be well read. May they be approached with the same deliberate care and skill that a child takes in sounding out an unfamiliar word. May they be read aloud and pondered with the appreciation and surprise that a teacher affords an apple on the desk. May they reinspire the wisdom of our youth and nudge us to speak it well.

Bridget Haase, O.S.U.
Dedham, Massachusetts
October, 2000

Life

" I'm really happy. I got a little bit of everything I want. "

—ISIDRO, 7

"Just when you're down on your luck, spring flowers bloom."—KYLE, 13

"When I sit by the ocean, I always tell God he really does give us the best he's got."

—JEAN EVA, 10

"You don't have to live with all the suffering you make for yourself."—LOUISA, 11

"A perfect spring day is God's way of reminding me that I'm tired of bowling."—RICARDO, 12

"Life's one thing you can't do alone."

—LORETTA MARY, 11

"God needs us to help people carry heavy things like books and tables. But sometimes life's a big load, too."—ALVAN, 10

"People say nature talks. All it tells me is that I have allergies."—HANK, 10

"Sometimes when I'm walking by myself I get this funny question inside. I mean—what makes me, me? My mirror doesn't answer."—BERNIE, 9

"Listen to the flowers. They tell you that even the worst things will brighten up."—CEREK, 12

Ida Jean

Ida Jean calls Dog Lick Hollow in the hills of Appalachia her home. She lives in a three-room house with her mother, seven brothers and sisters, and a host of stray animals taken in because they needed a home.

I first met Ida when she repeated third grade. She sat shyly in the back of the room with little reason to look up. Her school records contained a single sentence of evaluation: "She hain't learned nothin'."

That was far from true. She could call trees by name and knew when a "growin' shower" was coming by the feel of the wind on her face. She anticipated when tango gut would bloom in the hills and would gather it before it was gone. Ida Jean could smell a copperhead before she glimpsed it and tend a fire. She knew to plant potatoes in the dark of the moon and to cut hair in its last quarter.

Indeed, Mother Earth was her teacher. Ida Jean watched her every move, learned from her and confided in her as one confides in an imaginary friend.

Ida Jean did learn to read and do math. She learned to tell time even though she lives in the present. She learned self-esteem when she taught others to read clouds.

One day, she proclaimed with a spring shower of pride, "Reckon when I'm growed I'll be a teacher."

What Ida Jean did not realize was that she had already become a teacher. She challenged me to pack up and put aside my school bag of academic evaluations, growth charts and personal criteria for a successful education. Her lessons taught me what parents and teachers often forget: a large part of education occurs after 3 P.M.

Fatou

Fatou lives in the bush of Senegal, West Africa. Life there is a raw, continuous challenge.

Although the village has a windmill, there are often winds, but no water. This means she has long walks to the one well with a heavy bucket filled at her return. She also has the chore of gathering the firewood, often a difficult task since there is only so much kindling for many families.

Then there is the daily heavy pounding of the millet.

At ten years of age, Fatou knows how to balance water and wood on her head and the demands of life in her heart. And she does so like a mystic, fully aware of the life that surrounds her.

When the moon is full, Fatou slips away to catch a glimpse of the nightly white bloom of the baobab tree, knowing she will gather and taste its fruit in the morning.

This free spirit hums as she walks along and takes time to admire the finch-sized bluebirds that manage to find a drop to drink in all the oddest of places.

In the rainy season, Fatou revels in a downpour. Mud oozing between her toes, she twirls, dances and sings in the refreshing rain. Throwing back her head, she opens wide her mouth and drinks from heaven's well.

Fatou's source of life and strength are in being, not doing.

Knowing Fatou stirred and prodded me to examine why I often trudge through a day's schedule oblivious to the signs of life around me. She taught me that, despite hardships and monotony, life is meant to be lived, not simply endured.

"I can't wait to go to my auntie's for summer vacation. Do you think these are my 'good old days'?"—HANS, 6

"Hain't creeks wonderful! After the hard rains, I sit on the bank and watch for good stuff to come floatin' down. Got me some new toys that way."—MAGGIE SUE, 9

"Sometimes life's confusing. Like getting called on to read out loud. You think you know where people are, but you really lost the place."—LEON, 9

"Seeing tulips is great. Then I'm sure spring is back in business."—ALICE, 9

"When I be a-blowin' on a dandelion pod, it takes me a world away." —CHERISE, 9

"Sometimes when I'm mad, life feels like a cocklebur. It kinda' sticks to me." —TELISA, 9

"It's not really raining. The sun just needs to cry." —RUBY, 5

"I wish I could live like I was a hundred, instead of just seven. Then I could relax and get 'Meals on Wheels'." —KIRBY, 7

"I'm like a detective. I've got all these clues about life but need to solve the mystery myself."

—CRISSY, 13

overty

"I know that being poor should be no more."

—KIMBERLY, 12

"Even though we can't make it so that nobody is poor, at least we can help to make it the best for them."—MERCY, 10

"My daddy and I were talking about the poor. He said that the bottom line is that we help the poor. Then I asked Daddy if the top line is that we love them."—REESE, 9

"Once I saw a poor person lying on the street. My dad said he should get on his feet. But I don't think he meant just stand up."—JACK, 9

"Sometimes I'm in my room, and my stepmom thinks I'm doing nothing. But I'm really putting myself in poor people's shoes."—GINGER, 12

"Poor people are some of the greatest people alive. I mean they work every single day to survive, and that takes courage." —BRADY, 9

"Once I walked right by a poor street person. I still don't understand why I didn't give her anything." —JUDY, 9

"What really makes a person poor? When you got ripped clothes or when you ruin your life?" —GUY, 8

"I think becoming poor is like slowing down your life so much it stops. Then you don't go nowhere." —ELDON, 11

"I'm still in the refugee camp. Do you remember what it's like for me here?" —GEBRE, 13

Sulemon

Sulemon, one of 12,500 Ethiopians in the refugee camp of Wad Hileau, Sudan, East Africa, proved to be a trustworthy friend. A starving child, he was the victim of the ravages of the famine. I knew that he would survive when the day came that he took the bowl of hot milk from my hands and sipped it himself. My tears of encouragement felt like birth pangs. He grew strong and, at nine years of age, became my interpreter as we went from tent to tent looking for the malnourished. Sulemon could speak Amharic, Arabic and a few words of English.

But it was his big, black eyes that taught me what I needed most to know. With a single glance they could speak the secrets and desires of those he called family. They would also write today's homework in big black letters on the chalkboard of my heart: "Bring an extra high-energy biscuit." "Smile and give her hope." "Let him know that tomorrow we will come again."

Every day, Sulemon would join six hundred other children for daily rations of corn porridge and hot milk. I still remember the day he began a chant of thanks to Allah as the large buckets of milk came into the feeding center. This starving child did not yet realize the world owed him food and it was his right to eat.

One day he changed life for the children in the desert. "You teach; we sing!" he exclaimed.

And so we did. We would wait for the gray rats to eat the crumbs from the Oxfam high-energy biscuits and lick the milk that lingered on the feeding mats. Then children would gather and classes begin. Simple things, like hygiene and a little English, caught their attention.

Only when Sulemon put on a sack stamped "Powdered Milk, Gift of the United States of America," took an empty plastic box from the Oxfam biscuits and began to beat this drum did music return to the lives of the children. His eyes—and theirs—conveyed an enthusiasm and strength I never knew could exist amid the tragedies of a drought and a civil war.

On a dark, windy morning, I left to go home to food, clean water and medical attention. In the distance he stood, my faithful friend's desperate tears baked by a morning heat that had yet to know the dawn. When Sulemon saw me in the truck, he came running to say goodbye.

We both knew we would never see each other again. He touched the sky with his hands and then touched my eyes. Through the pool of our tears, the message was spoken without a word: "When I meet Allah and you meet God, let us ask about one another."

Even now Sulemon's life remains relatively unchanged in his land of want. In my land of plenty, he challenges me to open my eyes to creative uses for the most ordinary of things and to bring song and prayer to the most debilitating and hopeless of situations. It is his trust in Allah and joy in life that continue to encourage me in my struggles with complacency, consumerism and compassion.

Mago

The manicured lawn and terraced landscape artistically frame Mago's new home. Specially designed by a renowned Midwestern architect, it represents the wealth of her family and the peace of suburbia. The three-car garage houses a Saturn for errands and a BMW for outings. The empty space is for Mago's car when she comes of age; until then, she parks her top-of-the-line mountain bike there. She eagerly anticipates her home's finishing touches—an outdoor pool and deck.

Mago's favorite pastime is mall shopping. It's important to keep up with what's new and with friends. Her weekly spending money is limitless and independent of her allowance.

"Kids are kids only once," her doting father says, "and later she can learn about wise shopping."

Academically, Mago, fourteen, is in the top 3 percent of the student body of her girls' private academy. Never neglecting her homework, she finds time for after-school math teams, history club and peer tutoring. Working harder than most, it is her parents' pride, not just her grades, that she wishes to maintain.

Life seemed settled and comfortable...until Global Awareness Week at the academy.

Mago listened intently as a returning Peace Corps volunteer spoke of his experiences and service abroad. The speaker's tales of people's communal struggle and survival in the midst of war and indigenous poverty captivated her. She had an overwhelming sensation that, although these events happened "way over there," she was part of the problem "over here."

Questions she sometimes had conveniently dismissed surfaced again: Does my life influence other people's lives? How come I have all that I do and others have almost nothing? Do the clothes on my back put burdens on the backs of child laborers in Asia?

Deep down she wanted to help others, but had never found the right outlet. This handy excuse no longer satisfying her, she decided to seek her mother's guidance to see how she could make a difference.

Mago was faithful to this decision. Over the next few months, she and her mother investigated service possibilities. They found a homeless shelter and together began to fix meals there. Over time, this gradually led to serving the meals and eventually to table conversations with people they called friends.

Mago made the problems of homelessness a personal concern and shared her feelings and knowledge with her peers. By the end of the semester, three classmates had joined her to serve at the shelter.

Mago took further steps. With ease, not fanfare, she began to observe her purchasing and eating habits. With charm and grace, she would approach managers of major department stores, inquiring about their clothing lines in relation to child labor practices. With bold

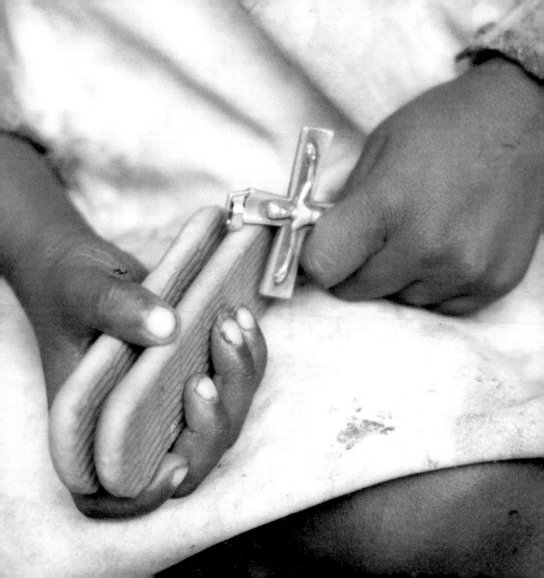

sincerity, she would ask supermarket heads about fruit and vegetable harvesting conditions. In a word, she began to think globally and not just about her own little world of designer jeans, CDs and bikes.

Speaking with Mago over the year, I realized that children do want to make a difference. They understand that even though they cannot solve society's many problems, they can at least do something about their choices. Open minds lead to open hearts. Adults label it "social consciousness"; children call it "caring."

Sulemon and Mago will never meet, but they both have gnawing hungers. Sulemon needs food; Mago wants to provide it. Perhaps his diet may one day improve because she watches hers. A little bit of awareness can start a quiet revolution.

"I never saw a poor person, but I keep asking God to let me meet one, 'cause I always keep a treat in my pocket for them."—LOWELL, 7

"I know Jesus said that when you do nice things, your left hand shouldn't know what your right hand is doing. Did he know how hard that is? When my right hand was putting money in the poor box, my left hand didn't know where to go."—COLBERT, 10

"I don't think 'poor' is a good word. It is in some ways but sometimes it isn't. I got called 'poor' once. I didn't know why. Maybe street people feel like that, too."—KATHRYN, 10

" I am rich when I go after what I need; but I'm real poor when I just keep a-wantin'. "

—DELLE MAE, 10

"I had lots of money in my piggy bank. My big brother broke it and threw my pennies all over the house. Now I have to look for them everyday after school. Because even my last penny belongs to the poor."—RAINA, 7

"I get confused about sacrificing my money for the poor. Sometimes I have extra but keep it in case I need it later on. Other times I see a poor person who could use it, but she doesn't seem good enough to get it."—TARAY, 13

"My neighbor thinks that hungry people who steal should be put in jail. But I think just thinking that is a crime."—BARRETT, 10

" Showing love is like giving a present you can always afford. **"**

—JAMAL, 11

Love

"Love is happening when someone you like passes by and a butterfly lands in your stomach at the same time."—TRESSA, 13

"Put two roses together and the smell's sweeter. That's how love is."—DORISA, 9

"We got to make love out of people's hurt pieces."
—CASSIE, 6

"I learned how to buy a dog. When you go to the pet store in the mall, you don't get the puppy that runs up and licks you all over. You watch the one in the back that's looking at you. You shouldn't make friends too fast."

—LIBBY, 8

"When you get married, two separate hearts get glued together in a new picture." —DAISY LOUISE, 7

"I got a certificate for being voted 'most Christian' in my class. Made me feel funny to get an award for trying to love." —SELENA, 12

"I came to visit my mama. It's hard to love her since I saw her kill my baby sister. My teacher said Jesus got killed, but he still loved. But I told her not by his mama. And it was just himself that got killed, not his sister." —TY, 9

"Loving costs, but it pays a lot, too." —BERWYN, 10

Julia

Julia, three, was dying of AIDS.

Each day, dressed in a new outfit—perhaps her mother's way of covering her guilt—she arrived at the HIV/AIDS day care. Deaf, blind and epileptic, Julia lived in a dark, silent world of seizures and pain. Her arms and legs flailed constantly as she tried to determine the boundaries of her external space.

We would carry her to the toddler's room and begin another day of total care and therapy. The other toddlers cuddled and hugged her in unconditional acceptance and joy in her presence.

After two years, her daily care became a challenge. The little improvement and even small victories, like sitting unsupported for a minute or two, failed to satisfy our need for major results. We wondered what her life was all about and our role in it. The demands of her medical conditions were exhausting, and we seemed fixed in a no-win, no-payback situation. Thoughts say it all, and ours spoke volumes.

Julia died on Thanksgiving Day. As families celebrated with feast and festive gatherings, Julia's mother sat alone, a single mother without family, enduring the loss of her only child and the pain of years of addiction.

As we grieved Julia's absence, we began to reflect on the meaning of her life, so fragile and short. We recalled the days it was diffi-

cult to continue our own self-giving love with its desires for rewards and compensations.

We shared simple memories: how peacefully she slept; how she relished yogurt taste by taste; how her physical aversion to touch slowly disappeared; how vital she was to our work at the day care; how empty the days now seemed without her.

In these moments we came to understand that she bestowed a gift on us that no child ever had. In her very dependence, she gave us, growing weak in our loving, the strength to continue each day. She reminded us that love is real even when it is sometimes not felt and hurts in its monotony.

In remembering Julia, we realized we needed her. Her physical weakness had become our inner strength. She had opened our blind eyes and deaf ears to the challenge of unconditional love. We came to believe that, even in the midst of doubt and painful questions, no act of love can be measured—nor is it ever wasted.

Josiah

Josiah, age four, is living with HIV/AIDS.

He is at home in the day care. Articulate and gifted, Josiah builds trucks and robots from Legos, enjoys reading about hungry caterpillars and deepwater sharks, and delights in dance and circle-time games. With a child's abandon, he hugs his purple Barney dinosaur, sings its love song and believes himself important.

Resilient and feisty, Josiah does not shy away from the challenges of his disease. He is learning to deal with his tube feedings as well as with wearing the backpack that contains his medicine infusions, vital to his survival. It hampers his playground adventures, but does not dampen his spirits. Bearing the emotional weight of parental separation anxiety, a result of his mother's death, he knows how to cry.

Yet with a sensitivity beyond his years, Josiah reaches out to others who seem to suffer more. Burdened, he laughs. Hurting, he consoles. Sick, he comforts. Learning to cope, he knows how to love.

Parental mistakes and poor choices have created lives for Josiah and many children like him that are neither fair nor easy. These mistakes have given a diminished quality to their lives. More tragically, those poor choices have placed adult burdens on small, fragile shoulders.

Surprisingly, these children have yet to learn the resentment and finger pointing that absorb others later in life. In their suffering, these children reflect the power of our inner resources. They are plugged in to the electricity of the present moment, not short-circuited by the "if only's" that adults so often have. Life may not be fair, but in their own simple way, these children try to level its playing field.

"Your heart knows when love is real."

—MIKAL, 11

"Love is like when you make music. Sometimes you strum it out and sometimes you dance it out."—JANICE, 8

"When you feel God's love, you're like a flower that blooms. You start slow and tight and then you open up. Others watch you and feel happy. And want love, too."—BRANDI, 10

"I was hugging my teddy bear when Mommy told me it was time to put it in the box for the poor. But sometimes you need a few extra minutes with something you love."—MILLICENT, 8

"Love is like a greeting from God. It's how he talks to us."—LUIS, 8

" It's this way with parents. If we don't have them, then they don't have us. **"**

—CIRO, 8

Famil

Y

"Family needs love and forgiveness. One makes good, and the other makes up."—WESTON, 13

"Sit on your mommy's lap while you can. You'll miss it when you're old."—TWAINA, 7

"What God has unionized, we should not break up."—GABRIELLE, 9

"My brother Pascal's in a wheelchair. We are the same except when we go places. Then I walk, and he rides."—MARCEL, 8

"You can't leave your childhood if your momma and daddy are still living."
—ANTON, 10

"A bride and groom make a promise that lasts for as long as they can take it."—DREW, 8

"You better watch out when you fight with your sister. When you get to be ninety, she might be all you got."—SERGIO, 8

"My mom has a big job teaching us kids to live right. All I learn from my dad is how to hit."
—CLAUDE, 8

Wynn

With a child's belief in the magic growth of beanstalks and other living things, Wynn, eight years old, has planted a sapling in his New York backyard that he hopes will yield a tree house. In the meantime, he spends most of his summer and after-school hours in the cave he made. Sheltered under a rock with side stacks of branches, twigs and pieces of lumber, Wynn constructed this hideout for doing what he loves most: reading, sketching and musing on dinosaurs.

Removing a book from his "bag of history," a name he has given his school bag, he studies one of these strange creatures with the eye of an artist and the precision of a scientist.

"You've got to really see them," he instructs, as he closes his book and begins to draw, "'cause your eyes can hold lots of details."

Wynn's life outside is far more peaceful than life inside. His father is usually in an alcoholic stupor and his stepmother fusses over the year-old baby that she considers her "real son."

Wynn has learned to fend for himself. He is usually a ten-o'clock scholar because he can't wake his dad for a ride to school; he skips breakfast, but knows he'll get a McDonald's hamburger for supper; and he's unkempt because the washing machine is still broken.

Wynn is confused by his father's drinking and worries about his smoking. He gave his dad a book from the school library about the dangers of cigarettes and even posted a sign "No drugs, cigarettes

or alcohol allowed in this house." He hasn't had any success but doesn't stop trying.

Wynn confessed through tears that there had been a major fight between his dad and his stepmom. He described the ugly details and then grew silent, exhausted by the painful memory. After a long while, he drew a deep breath, sighed and began.

"You know, even if my dad gets thrown out on the street and becomes homeless, even if he gets drunk and passes out on the sidewalk, I will still visit him everyday and take him food. No matter what, I will always love my dad."

The dependent, frightened love of a son filled the silence that followed.

Wynn reflected the immense conflict children often endure: the light and dark sides of parenting. Fathers and mothers long for the best in life for their children. And yet, their weaknesses can lead to their children's worst experiences of turmoil and struggle.

Suffering from his parents' choices, Wynn holds the love he has for his father as tightly as a teddy bear. It rises above the domestic shouts, stupors and neglect and becomes an amazing and saving grace.

Wynn carries on courageously, bravely and lovingly, knowing that, despite the heart-wrenching pain, he will always be his father's son.

Josefina

Josefina, eight, adores her parents. She knows that they are both hardworking and loving. Outside school hours, she shadows them, the lights of her life.

Some days, before the rooster crows, she accompanies her father and Popo, the family donkey, on milk deliveries. They walk slowly, greeting Ixtaccihuatl and Popocatepétl, the sleeping mountains of their Mexican village.

Again and again, her father recounts the folk tale of the forbidden love between the Toltec princess and the Chichimec prince. He tells of how the two enemy kings did not care about the dreams of their children. What Josefina cherishes most is that her father always asks about her dreams and promises to help fulfill them.

Sometimes her father points out all the "green gold" that Cortés left behind. Reminding her that it is the most important kind, he shows her the treasure of medicinal herbs and healing plants growing along the paths.

"Look to God for health," he says, "and then look under your feet."

It is not difficult for Josefina to look to the Divine, for she thinks God is just like her father.

Her mother's hands fascinate her. Rough and calloused with little spots and wrinkles, they become beautiful and graceful in making the day's tortillas. Josefina wonders if she'll acquire the skill of patting, flipping and baking them just right. As she watches her mother, she can begin to smell and taste them, served warm and oozing with cheese and beans.

Her mother hums as she works. When Josefina tells her that she sings sweeter than the birds, her mother beams, her eyes radiating unconditional love. Josefina feels bathed in warmth and light.

Nights are quiet and peaceful. Gathering around their home altar, the family lights the candles in honor of Our Lady of Guadalupe. With hands folded, or sometimes joined, each gives thanks and praise for the day. Together they sing a closing hymn to the glory of God and a good night song to La Virgencita.

Then each child kneels for a parental blessing. Josefina feels the strength of her father and the gentleness of her mother. Her father prays for her safety and good health; her mother, for guidance and peace. After long hugs, she snuggles in her warm bed and realizes that heaven has begun.

Unlike Wynn, who fends for himself, Josefina thrives in her close family bonds. Struggling to put one foot in front of the other, Wynn plods along alone. With a sure footing, Josefina walks hand in hand with others. Wynn yearns to know the difference family makes; Josefina experiences that it does. Each will always be someone's child. And perhaps, one day, someone's parent.

"We get one daddy to marry. Sometimes he dies. Then he becomes an angel. Daddies just keep going."—ARACELLI, 6

"My brother was born December 7. My granny was born December 8. And my dad was born December 9. Boy, talk about a chain reaction."
—DOMINIC, 9

"I hit my sister and then asked God to forgive me. I felt like when the Merry Maids came to clean my house."—CARLY, 7

"The reason people throw rice on brides is because everybody loves a good cook."—RITA, 7

"I turned off my nightlight yesterday. Mommy asked me what I was doing. I told her I was standing up to my fear."—JOHN, 8

"My brother lived first in my mommy. But he's more cuter now in real life."—JANIE, 5

"Do you think my daddy could be God's little brother? He's real good to me, and I think he learned it from God."—SERAPH, 6

"Once my mommy and I saw a shooting star at the same time. The things you share with your mommy are the memories you keep."
—MURIEL, 7

Edu

> **"** School reminds
> me that we're all
> still just learning.**"**
> —ADDISON, 10

cation

"School's like waking up in the morning. A slow start."—TIMMY, 9

"Learning's like both a roller coaster and a carousel. Sometimes it's up and down. Sometimes it's round and round."—NICOLA, 11

"School's either a prison for kids or a cheer for education. Depends on the teacher."—MARSHA, 11

"My teacher talks with her eyes. I can't read good, and she knows it. But when I try, she smiles and then winks at me. That means that one day I will."—LAVI, 11

"My teacher's words travel. They float out of his mouth and sink in my heart."—ZAIN, 12

"My teacher said that my eyes were as blue as the sky. I wish he would've noticed that the inside of my heart was, too."—RAUL, 12

"My stepmom taught me a real good lesson: Never cut someone else's hair unless you're a real barber."—FAWNA, 8

"It's always a mess at school on a secretary-less day."—ROBIN, 9

Doug

Close to the cornfields of Illinois, Doug struggled with his parents'
divorce and his mother's second marriage.

To complicate the situation, his stepbrother was in the same
sixth-grade class. Terrell was an outstanding student, accomplished
athlete and the apple of his father's eye. Doug found his studies a
challenge, wasn't too keen on sports, longed to play the flute and
take special art classes.

His family discouraged Doug's ambitions, deeming them unnec-
essary and counterproductive to an education. My conferences with
them were dead-ends.

At the end of the school year, the family moved to Arkansas. I said goodbye with sadness for I had failed to convince Doug's parents of his talents and gifts. Even as adults, they had not learned one of life's important lessons: It is acceptable to be different.

Two years passed. On a chilly March afternoon, I received a letter from Doug. Inside he had included a little plastic bag with small pieces of chalk. The letter began:

Dear Sister,

Remember how you used to ask me to wash the chalkboards and ledges? Well, I saved some of the colored chalk and put them in a special box I decorated. They meant a lot to me because you had held them in your hands. Last month, I used some of them to create an art project. It won first prize. So now I am sending you some little pieces back because I held these in my hands. This way we're in touch.

Your student always,
Doug

Closing the letter and resealing the plastic bag, I reflected on the hundreds of times I had written on the chalkboard. It took Doug to remind me that a teacher must write first on the hearts of her students with words of encouragement and acceptance. These words, written on flesh not slate, remain indelible and summon the power to shape a future.

Sasha

Across the Mississippi from Doug, Sasha faced a troubled adolescence of emotional outbursts and defiant behavior. She responded neither to disciplinary action nor positive reinforcement.

Repeated parental conferences were of little help. Her mother wondered how a child who had everything could lack anything. Her father insisted that he disciplined appropriately.

Sasha wandered lost and alone in an impenetrable world where adults were not welcomed.

Over the months, my frustration with her steadily increased. My patience as well as all the behavioral modifications objectively constructed by our counseling team were exhausted.

In late March, Sasha again incurred a penalty for a rule infraction. Called to my office, she sauntered in, silently challenging me as she looked me squarely in the eye and asked me what I wanted. In a flash, I raised my voice and exclaimed, "Nothing. I simply do not understand you. Nor do I want to. Now or ever."

Sasha winced. For the first time, a tear glistened which I noticed and she ignored. In a choking voice she responded, "Just because your eyes and ears are stuck in your head, doesn't mean you can't see and listen from deep down in your heart."

Then she began to cry.

That moment I understood. Sasha was a mystery. Deep, incom-

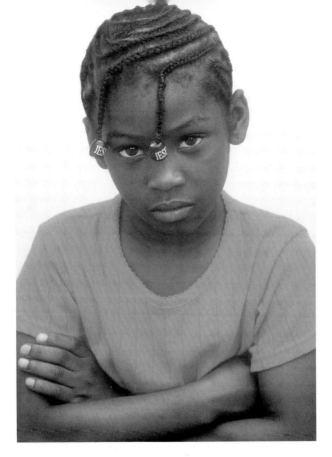

prehensible, unfolding, struggling, yearning to be accepted. I had made her into a problem to be measured, dealt with, solved and controlled. Stuck in my head, I had failed to feel her heart.

"Yesterday was some day at school. All of a sudden, the wind blew up, it got dark, and hail balls fell. Even the lights went out. My teacher told us to stay in our seats and don't move. But I think God wanted us to enjoy the show he was putting on."—FRANK, 11

"I want to stay in first grade all my life. My teacher says I have to move on. I guess I'll have to take everything with me."—RUBEN, 7

"School and the earth seem alike to me. They both revolve around something bigger."
—SIDNEY, 10

"My teacher really fussed at me today. But it was OK 'cause her eyes were smiling."
—COLTON, 6

"He never told me why, but after just nine lessons, my music teacher fired me." —CHANTILLY, 8

"The best words my teacher ever spoke were 'School's out!'"—EDLIN, 10

"The difference between being smart and being wise is like the difference between a light bulb and a star in the sky. The light bulb has a switch but the star has God."—THADDEO, 12

Futur

" Grow up slow.
It's too much to
handle all at once. **"**

—SHANNON, 8

"It's a job being six. You gotta' grow up to be seven, and I don't know nothin' about it."—ELISE, 6

"I want to be a dancer when I grow up. But I want to be a nurse, too. Maybe I could start something new at the hospital and be a dancing nurse."

—TAMMY, 7

"I'm either going to be an architect or a chef. I don't know yet because I'm waiting for God's decision."—ROSANNA, 8

"When I get big, I'll be an artist. I'll paint all the world leaders shaking hands together. Maybe if people see it, they would believe it could happen."—KATRI, 11

Alexia

Alexia, nine, does nothing half-heartedly.

Over the past few months, she has been growing cotton in her Louisiana backyard. She wants to expand her class project on Eli Whitney and the cotton gin to include specimens of her crops, posters of the development of cotton into cloth, and hopes, with the help of her neighbor, to design and make an all-natural cotton skirt.

By the time she was eight years old, Alexia had created her own country, somewhere in the Far East, with its own customs, flag and native dress. She had mapped out the borders and cities, and practical ways people would share their natural resources with neighboring countries. She taught her circle of friends the made-up language so they could read the folk tales she was beginning to write. Enthralled with geography, she decided on this project for after-school fun.

For Alexia, life is one giant journey toward the future. In an old notebook, with other treasures under her bed, she has listed all the places she hopes to visit. She says that to meet a goal, one needs to be specific. So she has put down by what age and date she will have toured each country. With a broad smile and tales of discovery and adventure, she'll show you that she has already checked off Mexico.

Alexia is convinced that she can be and do anything she wishes.

She takes karate for concentration and never wears pink on principle. She is afraid to be branded "just a girl" because labels can lead to limits.

With an extraordinary sensitivity for the rights and needs of others, she has jotted down some things to remember in case she becomes president and is challenged to help solve society's problems. Occasionally, she adds a memo to a world leader with advice on peace and justice.

Alexia keeps the windows and doors of her future wide open. With a child's exuberance, she revels in its endless possibilities. She believes that everything is within her grasp; nothing is beyond her reach. She is confident that her dreams will become reality.

Reflecting on Alexia's life, I examine mine with its adult tension between realism and dreams. Having experienced life's disillusionment and struggled with its constraints, I have tempered my dreams. Because I have kept doors merely ajar and closed windows of opportunity too quickly, I have lost some of creativity's invigorating fresh air and passion.

Alexia taught me to let realism yield to hope. Her enthusiasm still challenges and encourages me to return to the treasures underneath my bed, reread lists of childhood dreams and breathe deeply of potential and possibility.

Lil' William

Since the age of five, Lil' William, son of Big William, has worked the Kentucky fields. He has a love affair with the land.

His days follow the planting and harvesting routine with extra sleep and a bit of schooling snatched during off-seasons. He rises early, preferring the cool morning hours and the feel of the damp soil under his bare feet. But he takes the heat of the day in stride. "No sun, no crops, no money, no food," he says, sweating and flashing teeth stained by tobacco, a witness that the land has become part and parcel of who he is.

By age seven, Lil' William could teach how to chew tobacco ("safer than matches in dry weather") and how to cut it. Cutting is laboring work and limited tools challenge him to do the best he can with what he has. His skill allows him to keep pace with older children and even a few adults. With pride he'll point out his harvest, hanging in the barn to dry.

His father's long absences put family responsibilities on this child's shoulders and adult thoughts of the future in his young mind. In many ways, Lil' William is already a little man.

His dedication to the fields is evidence of his hope for a better life. Like Alexia, Lil' William dreams of the future. He plans on buying a few acres, planting and harvesting as he wants. He feels that being his own boss would give him more choices and that taking charge of

his life is the key to improving it.

"The land is my friend," he says. And then adds, "It always gives me hope."

Both Alexia and Lil' William are children with goals and hopes. One stands on her front lawn and looks out on the whole world; the other stands amid tobacco leaves and longs for a piece of land.

The future is both a challenge and a mystery. Until it is upon us, it keeps secret the crossroads and detours of our journeys. It may cause the ground to shift under our feet, causing our hopes to sway and our dreams to totter.

Alexia and Lil' William teach us that potential and possibility can ground and sustain us. They remind us that goals inspire and hopes renew. And when the realities of adulthood discourage us, passion for what lies ahead keeps us putting one foot in front of the other.

"*I like growing up because that means I have less time in this hard, cruel world.*"—JORY, 14

"Watch out when you get out of bed in the morning. You just don't know what's going to hit you in the face."—JOZEF, 9

"*It's hard to keep going when you don't know what's coming.*"—SHERMAN, 9

"Lots of times I wonder if the road ahead will have lots of bumps in it. But I guess ruts would be worse."—SERENA, 11

"The future's like a brand new book. The cover's so exciting you want to dive right in. But you know it's the story that counts and the ending can throw you for a loop."—RYE, 13

> **"**I was with Gram when she died. I saw that life is good to the last drop.**"**
>
> —TABETHA, 10

Deat

h

"When you die, you go to God's castle. The door's wide open, but you have to walk in with Jesus."

—DARYL, 7

"My mommy was sad because my papa died. I told her Jesus would get her over it because there's more to life than crying."—JORGE, 10

"I'm so sad my baby brother died. He never got to walk or talk. But now he'll get to grow up with God."—VIOLET, 7

"When my grammy died, her soul went to heaven. And her body went in a big treasure chest. Now that's cool!"—SAMSON, 5

"Heaven is the best place to go, so I don't care when I die. Except not before Christmas."

—CURTIS, 8

Crystal

Crystal, eight, lives in rural Maine, under the spell of the ocean. Sitting on rugged rocks, she smells it in the air, feeling its breeze cool her face and mess her hair. Just she and Grampy.

She adored Grampy. He would meet her after school and together they would begin their explorations. Some days they were shell-seekers; other days, they were "snake-eyes," as he would say.

Grampy seemed to know everything about seashells: their names, shapes and even their origins. But the way he held each one taught Crystal more. He would hold a shell reverently, marvel at its beauty, share his knowledge, then put it back in the sand. "It's home here," he would say.

It was the same way with snakes. In the late spring and summer, Crystal and Grampy would find little fields and begin their search to discover a new species, size or color. He taught her how to let them glide smoothly in her hands, like fish in the ocean. She laughed when her best friends said they were too busy to go snake hunting. She knew they were afraid of them.

One hot summer morning, Crystal discovered a new rock haven along the shore. "Just big enough for the two of us," she excitedly told Grampy.

"And the perfect place for sharing our secrets," he whispered with a touch of sadness in his voice.

They climbed together, safely nestling in the water-worn shelter. With its rocky fastness protecting his heart, Grampy knew that he had to tell her. He was sick, he said. He had cancer.

Then he pointed out the horizon and said that beyond it were big ships. He knew that, even though he could not see them. Grampy asked Crystal to believe it, too. He reassured her that heaven's like that, real but unseen. He told her he would have a long time to glide peacefully in God's sea of love, just like fish and snakes. They held hands and sat a long time, the sound of the waves adorning the silence between them.

Three months later, Crystal came downcast into the classroom.

"He's gone," she said quietly. And then continued, "I think Grampy knew when God was coming because he was real relaxed. Like when we were together by the ocean. I don't know when God got there, but Mommy did. I'm sure he will always keep the present I gave him. I gave him all my tears to take with him."

I opened my arms and embraced Crystal like the ocean around a jutting rock.

How often have I repressed, choked on, excused, fought and hidden my tears. Somehow I would feel less adult, too emotional and very unheroic if they would fall. Crystal reminded me that tears are a gift, given and received.

Like the tide, thoughts of Crystal roll in when I gaze at the ocean's horizon with the shells of loved ones' memories at my feet.

Nicky

Nicky, fourteen, only wanted to keep his brothers and sisters together as a family.

One of four children, each with a different father, Nicky and his siblings were homeless city children, moving from place to place on the north side of St. Louis, Missouri. In and out of different schools, they were overlooked by the educational system, and received most of their knowledge from the streets.

Nicky's mother, a drug addict, was serving eighteen months for possession. His natural father had long since disappeared. The children were placed in foster homes, separated, alone and missing each other.

Soon after placement, Nicky ran away from foster care. He lived on the streets and found a job working ten hours a day at a car wash. Little by little, convinced that he could persuade his father to reunite and care for the family, Nicky hoped to save enough money to find him.

On a sweltering August day, a middle-aged business man came to the car wash, talked a little with Nicky, tipped generously and made Nicky an offer he could not refuse.

The man agreed to pay Nicky $20,000 to shoot a drug dealer. He would even provide the gun. He explained to Nicky that money would no longer be a problem and that he and his siblings could enjoy a home and food. It was an easy plan to make his dream come true.

The next week, Nicky followed instructions, sought the victim out and pulled the trigger. He never realized that the death would be the beginning of his own.

Expected to be tried as an adult with a twenty-year state prison term, he was sent to the City Juvenile Detention Center before trial.

Every child loves a birthday. Nicky's came around, but no one noticed. He wrote a touching letter and asked the detention center chaplain to deliver it. He began:

Dear God,

> *Today's my birthday but no one knows or even cares. You made the sky with all the stars so I know you remember you made me. Wish we could talk stuff over but this is the best I can do. Chap said you'd get this letter.*
>
> *I'm so alone here, God. Is this like when we die? Chap said you'd understand, but I need more than that.*
>
> *Can you help me, God?*

Sincerely,
Nicky

After reading the letter, I asked myself, Who cries harder? The child who suffers, or the adult who suffers with the child?

There are children who know death before they have truly known life. Some learn about death with a Grampy at the ocean; some learn about it in a prison lock-up, wondering why, in trying to better their lives, their life begins to shut down.

Whether reflecting before a vast horizon or in a narrow cell behind bars, death remains an intimidating mystery that we often flee in terror. Accepting it with tears and regret, we are challenged to turn and face it squarely. Only then will it release its fearful grip and set us free.

"This song in church says that heaven's streets are all gold. Reckon it's worth one trip there to find out."
—ELLIOT, 9

"The worst thing about death is that you're never seen alive again."—ANTWAN, 8

"My nana died soon after the priest read her the last rights."—VONNIE, 12

"I asked my mommy if Santa ever dies. She said not if people love others and share. But I don't know. That long gray beard's got me worried."—REX, 6

"Heaven's a super place but it's not like earth. Do you think I'll hurt God's feelings if I get just a little homesick?"—BRENDAN, 7

"If heaven's all they say it is, we better never take it lightly."—LILLIAN, 13

God

"God is as good as it gets."

—CURT, 9

"You never know what God has in mind. He likes to keep lots of stuff a surprise."—BRADLEY, 8

"No matter what, God will always be my One and Only."—LEA, 11

"God and the Easter Bunny work together. Only God knows if you're really sleeping or just faking. Then he tells the Bunny."—GIA, 5

"If you keep telling your conscience to go away, one day it won't come back."—SALANA, 10

"What Jesus said to Martha was simple: 'Have faith in me and forget the housework.'"—MINDY, 10

"When I go outside and look around, God is always right in front of me."—YURI, 9

"I think God gives all of us the same amount of talent. We just don't know how to measure it."
—MIKE, 13

"God made us because he wanted to have neighbors."—HOWARD, 9

"God uses us in all ways. It's called his plan. The problem is when he keeps it all a secret."
—BENNY, 8

"Some people think God is like a ruler who calls the shots. But I think he's like a coach who helps me learn the game."—THEODORE, 12

Roma Child

I never knew her name. She was a young child in Rome standing forlorn and cold outside the train station. In her arms she carried a toddler, naked, dirty and hungry. From time to time this ten-year-old would glance lovingly at her and stroke her head.

After a year in Rome, I knew the ways of the street children. They would often distract an unsuspecting tourist to steal from them. From afar I studied this girl, as if she were a great Italian work of art. Even in her unkemptness, she radiated depth, dignity and grace. I wondered if she was waiting for a passerby or just waiting for time to pass.

Not sure why, I approached her, clutching my purse as tightly as she grasped her sister. Our eyes met and I, surprising both her and myself, offered my lunch bag. She put her sister down, gently and gingerly took the sack, and began to unpack its contents: bread, cheese, an apple and a piece of chocolate. Her eyes brightened and I was pleased with my courage and charity.

The girl took a bite out of the apple and, much to my chagrin, began to repack the lunch. Feeling disheartened and wrestling with resentment I thought, Why did I bother? The poor can be so choosy. Putting the lunch on the ground, she picked up her sister. I knew she was leaving both it and me.

Then she looked at me with a smile as wide as the Coliseum.

With tenderness she held out her sister. Her eyes and her nod bade me take her. Reaching for her, I held her close.

In charity, a first-world adult shared bread to feed; in love, a poor street child shared life to nourish and nurture. The famous paintings and ornate monuments, the magnificence of Rome's churches and the power of its history paled before this graced encounter. This child was life's masterpiece. Without a word spoken, she invited me to contemplate the canvas of a work in progress. And before God's work of art called a human life, the only response is reverence, silence and love.

"I saw this picture in church. I knew right away it was Jesus because he looked just like his Father."

—RENE, 7

"Once in God's family, you are in it for life. God loves us too much to let us go."—VERA MARIE, 10

"This is what happens when I pray. My heart goes up and God's heart comes down and we meet smack in the middle."—NANCY, 8

"Sometimes I really don't care about loving people. Then when I go to talk to God I get static on the line."—LEVEY, 11

"Sometimes my heart's words become a song to God. That's called prayer."—ESTELLE, 11

"Listen real good to your granny's prayers. They'll be the first thing you think of when you get old and need God."—LADONNA, 8

"If God came to talk to me, he'd probably wink and ask, 'How's life going without me?'"—LARIEN, 13

"Jesus loved to pray. That's how come he snuck off to the temple. But he still should've told his mother."—LARRY, 10

God knew the only way to share his heart was to make me."—MARI, 8

"When I think about how much God loves me, it is breathtaking."—JULIETTE, 10

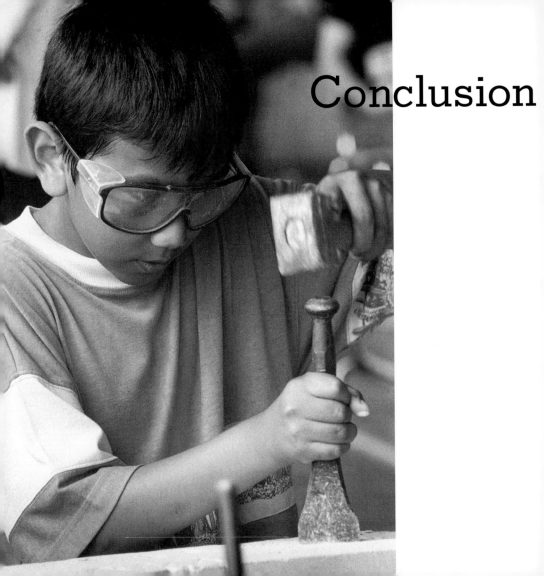

Conclusion

Fatou, Josefina, Mago and countless children like them have taught me in ways I never dreamed possible.

With characteristic clarity and crispness, magic and grace, they see and experience reality unobstructed by the adult obstacles of pride and prestige. Their simple insights have sometimes erased my preconceived notions, motivated me to change and taught me to laugh at myself. They have awakened me from my adult daydreams and invited me to experience a world I have long outgrown.

In their words and actions, children, standing only a short while on the pillars of time, ask us to examine what holds us up and holds us together. From their vantage point, they reveal vistas of life and love that we encounter every day yet take for granted. They challenge us to live with eyes wide open and hearts full of compassionate love.

Sulemon eyed a drum in an empty box and brought music to a desert feeding center. His joy made us family.

Julia's blindness opened our eyes to see that self-giving love is never lost. Her dependence made us strong.

Lil' William looked out on a field and saw a future. His optimism gave us hope.

Nicky peered through bars of a jail cell and sought God. His suffering brought us to prayer.

By pondering their lives and words, we not only return to a world of apples and crayons, of notebooks and lunch programs. We also go on a great treasure hunt. Grabbing our hands, children lead us from our heads to our hearts, from the playground of education to an interior classroom, a secret hideout where wisdom is spoken so well.

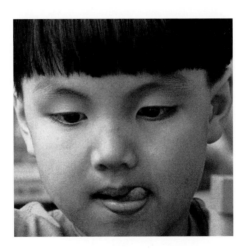